GREEN CRAFTS

Cool Crafts

with

Newspapers, Magazines, and Junk Mail

by Jen Jones

green projects for Resourceful Kids

CAPSTONE PRESS
a capstone imprint

Snap Books are published by Capstone Press,
151 Good Counsel Drive, P.O. Box 669, Mankato, Minnesota 56002.
www.capstonepub.com

 Books published by Capstone Press are manufactured with paper
containing at least 10 percent post-consumer waste.

Library of Congress Cataloging-in-Publication Data
Jones, Jen.
  Cool crafts with newspapers, magazines & junk mail : green projects for resourceful kids / by Jen
Jones.
    p. cm.—(Snap. Green crafts)
  Includes bibliographical references and index.
  Summary: "Step-by-step instructions for crafts made from old newspapers, magazines, and junk
mail and information about reusing and recycling"—Provided by publisher.
  ISBN 978-1-4296-4764-9 (library binding)
  1. Paper work—Juvenile literature. 2. Salvage (Waste, etc.)—Juvenile literature. I. Title. II.
Series.
  TT870.J664 2011
  745.54—dc22
                    2010002276

Editorial Credits

Lori Shores, editor; Juliette Peters, designer; Sarah Schuette, photo stylist;
    Marcy Morin, project production; Laura Manthe, production specialist

Photo Credits

All photos by Capstone Studio/Karon Dubke except:
Jen Jones, 32
Shutterstock/Amy Johansson (chain link fence); Ian O'Hanlon (recycling stamp)

Essential content terms are **bold** and are defined at the bottom of the page
where they first appear.

Printed in the United States of America in North Mankato, Minnesota.
102010
005987R

Table of Contents

6

10

14

16

22

24

Introduction

Believe it or not, you'll probably use about 18 tons (16 metric tons) of paper in your lifetime. You will also likely receive 560 pieces of junk mail every year. And that's not counting all those fashion magazines piling up in your room! If that sounds like a lot of wasted paper, you're right. But there's good news too. By reusing materials, you can make a big difference to the **environment**. And the great news is that being green can be fun!

Get ready to get creative because soon you'll be turning old paper into new, cool crafts. You won't be just keeping paper out of the **landfill**. You'll be making useful and attractive items of which you can be proud. Turn junk mail into a nifty notepad or transform newspaper into jazzy jewelry. Talk about turning trash into treasures!

environment—the natural world of the land, water, and air
landfill—an area where garbage is stacked and covered with dirt

Go Metric!

It's easy to change measurements to metric! Just use this chart.

To change	into	multiply by
inches	centimeters	2.54
inches	millimeters	25.4
feet	meters	.305
yards	meters	.914

Did You Know?

Keeping paper out of the landfill is important, but there are other benefits to recycling. Recycling uses less energy than it takes to make paper from raw materials. As a result, the process produces less air pollution. And one ton (0.9 metric ton) of recycled paper saves 17 trees.

recycle—to make used items into new products

Future Dreamin'

Do you dream of visiting Paris? Dating that guy down the block? Getting a cute, cuddly pup? Capture your goals and dreams in one beautiful **collage** with this easy vision board. Include places to go, people to meet, goals to achieve—the sky's the limit! Vision boards are popular with the A-list crowd, with fans ranging from President Obama to Oprah. These people believe that creating a picture of what you want makes things more likely to happen. So think big and go forth with glue stick in hand!

Here's what you need:
- **magazines**
- **scissors**
- **poster board, any size**
- **glue stick**
- **markers (optional)**
- **stickers (optional)**

Step 1
Flip through some old magazines to find pictures and words that represent things you'd like in your life.

Step 2
Cut out images and words to include on your vision board.

Step 3
Arrange the images any way you like on a piece of poster board.

Step 4
Glue the images to the poster board one at a time.

Step 5 *(not pictured)*
If you want, use markers to write things that are important to you, like "family." Or add stickers for a finishing touch.

Tip: You can also make a gratitude board to show the things for which you're grateful. It's a fun way to give thanks, which will help you attract more good stuff into your life!

collage—a variety of pictures or words cut out from magazines and glued onto a separate piece of paper

It's a Wrap

Wrapping paper and shopping bags generate 4 million tons (3.6 million metric tons) of trash every year in the United States alone. Yet there's still reason to celebrate. You can do your part to save the planet by creating your own rockin' wrapping paper! Friends and family will love the stylish look of this **eco-friendly** gift that keeps on giving.

Here's what you need:
- **small gift box**
- **newspaper**
- **scissors**
- **magazines**
- **glue stick**

How to Wrap a Gift

Place the gift face down on the paper. Wrap the paper around the gift and tape the ends of the paper together at the center.

Turn the box so one unwrapped side is facing you. Fold the left and right side flaps in toward the center. Press and smooth the paper down flat over the edges of the gift. Fold the bottom flap up to the center. Fold the top flap to the center and tape down. Repeat on the other unwrapped side of the gift.

1

Step 1

To figure out how much wrapping paper you'll need, place a small gift box on a sheet of newspaper. Cut a square big enough to cover the box by folding ends up and over the top. The paper should overlap by about an inch.

Step 2

Look through some magazines for colorful pictures or ads. Cut out an image you like.

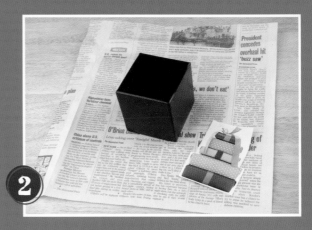

Step 3

Use a glue stick to attach the image face up on the newspaper.

Step 4

Continue cutting out images and gluing them to the newspaper. The pictures should overlap each other by about ½ inch. Cover the entire newspaper.

Step 5

Allow all the glue to dry before wrapping the gift.

Tip: Choose a theme that goes with the gift you're giving. Photos of interesting places are great for a travel bag. Pictures of popular musicians would go well with a CD.

eco-friendly—causing minimal or no harm to the environment

Boho Beads

If you love that earthy boho look, then these chunky paper beads are a perfect style fit! String them together to make bracelets, necklaces, and other fun **accessories**. But be warned—people might stop you on the street. They'll want to know where you got your fabulous jewelry!

Here's what you need:
- newspaper, 2 sheets
- large mixing bowl
- boiling water
- 2 tablespoons white glue
- toothpicks
- cookie sheet
- wax paper
- acrylic paint
- clear gloss sealer spray
- ¼ wide ribbon
- clear tape

Step 1
Rip newspaper into tiny pieces. Put the pieces into a large mixing bowl.

Step 2
Have an adult pour 1 cup boiling water over the newspaper in the bowl. Let the water cool for one hour, stirring every 10 minutes.

Step 3
Slowly pour out excess water from the paper. Squeeze the paper to remove as much water as possible and drain again.

Step 4
Add white glue to the paper. Mix with your hands until the paper sticks together in a large ball.

accessory—something that goes with your clothes, such as a belt or jewelry

To finish this project, turn to the next page. ⇨

Step 5 *(not pictured)*

Roll the paper into round beads of any size. If needed, add more glue to help the beads stick together better.

Step 6

Use a toothpick to poke a hole through one bead. Leave the toothpick in the bead.

Step 7

Place the bead on a cookie sheet covered with wax paper.

Step 8 *(not pictured)*

Repeat steps 6 and 7 with all beads.

Step 9

Allow the beads to dry for one week. Roll the beads between your palms three to four times each day so they don't develop a flat side.

Step 10

When the beads are completely dry, use acrylic or metallic paint to color the beads. Let paint dry.

Step 11

Take the beads outside and set them on newspaper. Spray with clear gloss sealer following the directions and safety tips on the can. Allow the beads to dry before removing the toothpicks.

Step 12

Roll one end of a piece of ribbon into a point. Use a small piece of clear tape to secure the end. Thread beads onto the ribbon, adding small knots between each bead. When enough beads are strung to make a bracelet or necklace, tie the ends of the ribbon in a knot and trim ends.

Tip: For a multi-colored look, apply two coats of paint in different colors. When the second coat is dry, use sandpaper to create a fun two-toned effect.

Artistic Notions

It's back-to-school time, and you're itching to unleash your creativity. Why not make your mark with a standout locker accessory of your own creation? Make your mark with this oh-so-pretty pencil holder.

Here's what you need:
- scissors
- magazine
- glass jar, clean with labels removed
- craft glue
- acrylic paints
- paintbrush
- glue gun and hot glue
- ribbon, long enough to wrap around jar

Step 1
Cut out a magazine photo no bigger than the size of the glass jar.

Step 2
Apply glue to the edges on the front of the image. Place it flat against the inside of the jar. Let dry.

Step 3
Use acrylic paints to coat the inside of the jar except where the picture is glued. Use one color or several colors. Let dry.

Step 4
Hot glue a ribbon around the rim of the jar and tie the ends in a bow. Trim off ends of the ribbon.

Tip: Feel free to use more than one picture. Space a few pictures around the jar or use smaller images to make a collage.

Pocket Books

Between school, family, and friends, it can be tough to keep track of your to-do list. You can keep everything in one easy place with this pocket-sized notepad. Because it's made of junk mail, you can make as many as you need.

Here's what you need:
- ruler
- scissors
- thin cardboard
- junk mail letters, one-sided
- junk mail envelopes
- stapler
- markers

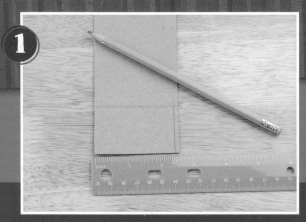

1

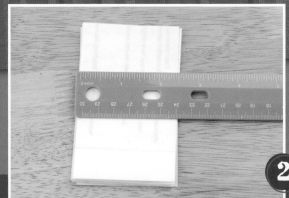

2

Step 1
Measure and cut out a 1½ inch by 2½ inch piece of thin cardboard.

Step 2
Using junk mail letters and envelopes, measure and cut out 15 pieces of paper that are 4 inches long by 2½ inches wide.

Step 3
Fold the cardboard in half so it is ¾ inch wide by 2½ inches long.

Step 4
Place the junk mail pieces inside the fold with the blank sides facing up. Make sure the sides of the paper stack are even.

Step 5
Bind the notepad together by stapling twice across the top.

Step 6
Use markers to decorate the top of your new notepad.

Tip: Why stop at just junk letters? Rock out the recycling and use old school papers with printing on only one side. Just make sure your parents see your papers first!

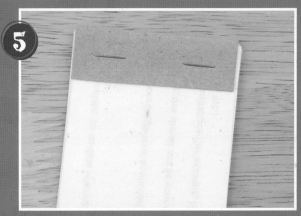

Funny Gifts

The Sunday comics are good for more than just a laugh. They can also make a cute gift bag! Just make sure whoever gets the gift actually opens it. After all, he or she might get stuck reading the comics.

Here's what you need:

- 1 23-inch by 22-inch sheet of newspaper comics, folded to 23 inches by 11 inches
- ruler
- tape
- 2 thin-cardboard boxes, such as a cereal or cake mix box
- scissors
- pencil
- white glue
- hole punch
- 2 pieces of ribbon, 20 inches long

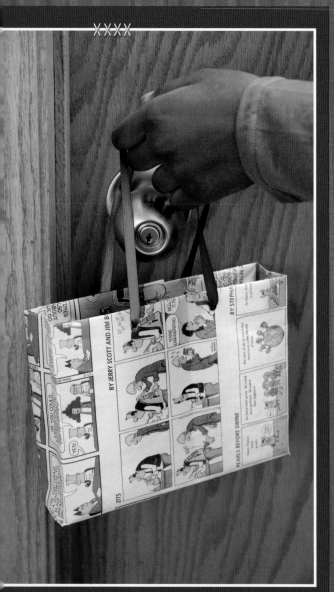

Step 1

Lay the newspaper flat with the folded edge at the top. Fold the top edge over by 1 inch. Tape down the entire folded edge.

Step 2

Wrap the newspaper around a small box so it overlaps by 1 inch at the center of the box. Cut away any paper beyond the 1-inch mark and tape the overlapped edge down. Make sharp folds along the edges of the box.

Step 3

Fold and tape the paper together at the bottom of the box as you would when wrapping a present. (See gift wrapping instructions on page 8.) Do not tape the paper to the box. Make sharp folds along the bottom edges.

Step 4

Slide the box out from the paper and set on a piece of cardboard. Trace around one side of the box and cut out. Apply a thin layer of glue to one side of the cardboard and place at the inside bottom of the gift bag.

Step 5

Bring the top edges of the bag together by folding the side edges to the inside. Make sharp folds about halfway down the bag.

Step 6

On one side of the bag, make two holes ½ inch from the top edge and 3 inches apart. Thread ribbon through the holes from outside to inside and tie knots to secure. Repeat on other side of bag.

Tip: You don't have to limit yourself to the Sunday comics. Get creative and use other sections of the paper too!

19

Jazzy Journal

Why spend your money on a fancy journal when you can make one at home? This project turns a plain composition book into the jazziest journal around. There's just one problem. It's so cute, you won't want to keep it a secret!

Here's what you need:

- ruler
- scissors
- magazines
- glue stick
- toothpick
- photo, cut to
    3 inches tall by
    4 inches wide
- craft glue
- composition notebook

1

2

Step 1
Measure and cut 106 squares of colorful magazine paper about 3 inches in size.

Step 2
Use a glue stick to apply glue diagonally from corner to corner on the back side of one square.

Step 3
Starting at one glued corner, tightly roll the square around a toothpick to form a tiny tube. Hold the end down for a few seconds to secure. Snip a bit off the ends of the tube so that they are flat.

Step 4 *(not pictured)*
Repeat steps 2 and 3 with all of the magazine pieces.

Step 5
Center and glue a 3- by 4-inch photo on the cover of a composition notebook.

Step 6
Use craft glue to attach 11 tubes vertically on either side of the photo. Glue each tube close to the previous tube so the notebook cover doesn't show through.

Step 7
Glue the remaining 84 tubes on side by side, to cover the front of the notebook. Let dry.

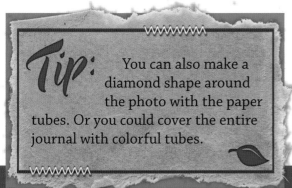

Tip: You can also make a diamond shape around the photo with the paper tubes. Or you could cover the entire journal with colorful tubes.

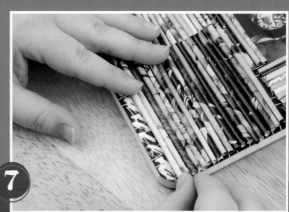

Flower Power

Besides planting the seed for smart recycling, paper flowers are sure to brighten up any room. These flowers are so easy, they'll have your room blooming in no time! And with the **templates** you'll make in this project, you can have flowers anytime you want.

Here's what you need:

- **3 pieces of thin cardboard, such as from a cereal box**
- **pencil**
- **ruler**
- **scissors**
- **white glue**
- **junk mail letters**
- **wax paper**
- **acrylic paint**
- **thin twigs, about 8 inches long**

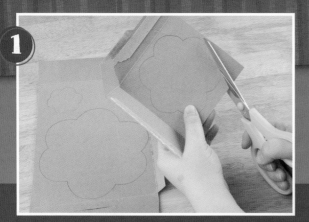

1

2

Step 1

Draw three flowers on pieces of thin cardboard. Make one flower about 2 inches wide. Make the second flower about 4 inches and the last flower about 6 inches. Cut them out to make tracing templates.

Step 2

Glue two pieces of junk mail together. Trace a flower template onto the junk mail and cut out. Repeat with other two templates.

Step 3

Place the flowers on wax paper. Paint the front and back of each flower any color. Let dry.

Step 4

Cut a 2-inch square from a piece of junk mail. Apply a thin layer of glue halfway across one edge. Place a thin twig on the glued section of the edge. Tightly roll the square into a tube around the twig. Glue down the edge and let dry.

Step 5

Paint the open end of the tube any color. You can paint the rest of the tube and twig green if you want.

Step 6

Cut a small hole in the middle of each flower. Slide the open end of the tube through the hole in each flower piece, from largest to smallest. Leave the colored ½ inch of the tube showing at the front.

Tip: If you're longing for flowers in the winter, but can't find any twigs, fear not! Use green pipe cleaners or longer paper tubes for stems.

template—a shape or pattern that you draw or cut around to make the same shape in another material

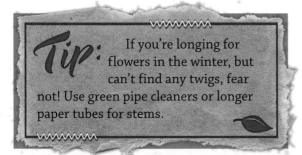

Bowl-tastic

Tidy up your desk or dresser with these stylish bowls. Use **papier-mache** to make them any size you want. Papier-mache can be used to make just about anything! After making these bowls, you're sure to find new ways to use papier-mache.

Here's what you need:
- newspapers, for covering work area
- small plastic bowl
- balloon
- newspapers, for making project
- papier-mache paste
- scissors
- acrylic paint

How to make papier-mache paste
Place two cups of water and one cup flour in a bowl. Stir well. The paste should be runny like glue. Add more water or flour, a little at a time, if necessary. Stir well to remove lumps.

Step 1
Cover your workspace with newspaper. Place a small plastic bowl on the newspaper.

Step 2
Blow up a balloon and tie the open end shut. Place the balloon in the bowl so it is steady.

Step 3
Tear off a strip of newspaper and dip it into the papier-mache paste.

Step 4
Remove the strip from the paste. Press out any extra paste by running your fingers down the length of the strip.

FACT!
Papier-mache means "chewed-up paper" in French.

papier-mache—paper that has been soaked in glue

To finish this project, turn to the next page. ⇨

Step 5
Lay the strip over the round top of the balloon.

Step 6
Repeat steps 3 through 5 until the top half of the balloon is completely covered by newspaper strips. Let dry.

Step 7 (not pictured)
Repeat steps 3 through 6 to add more layers. Make the bowl as thick or thin as you like by adding between five and 15 layers of paper. Let dry.

Let your eco-style show by only painting one side of the bowl.

Step 8
Use scissors to pop the balloon. Carefully peel the balloon pieces away from the papier-mache bowl.

Step 9
Trim the edges of the bowl.

Step 10
Apply two coats of paint to both the inside and the outside of the bowl. Let dry.

Tip: Papier-mache paste can get a little stinky. Add a little cinnamon into your papier-mache paste to say good-bye to the smell!

Green Crafting Facts

🐞 When writing in your notebook or printing papers, be sure to use both sides of the sheet. And don't leave a paper trail. Remember to recycle any old papers or research materials.

🐞 If your school doesn't have a recycling program, consider starting one. You can help reduce the 38 tons (34.5 metric tons) of paper thrown away by schools every single year.

🐞 Every year, U.S. businesses throw away enough paper to build a 12-foot (3.6-meter) wall that stretches from New York City to Los Angeles. Junk mail plays a big part in all that waste. Put a stop to junk mail by signing the petition for a "Do Not Mail" registry online. The registry would allow people to decide whether they want to receive junk mail.

Instead of always buying books and magazines, you can borrow some from the library. Many libraries have a loan system to help you find books not available at your local library. You'll be lending a green hand by saving a few trees—and some hard-earned cash!

Recycled newspapers become tissue, packaging, and more. In 1989, just 35 percent of newspapers were recycled. Today that number has jumped to 73 percent. To help bring that number to 100 percent, make sure your family recycles the newspaper. Read all about it, and then recycle it!

Glossary

accessory (ak-SEH-suh-ree)—something that goes with your clothes, such as a belt or jewelry

collage (kuh-LAHZH)—a variety of pictures or words cut out from magazines and glued onto a separate piece of paper

eco-friendly (EE-koh-frend-lee)—causing minimal or no harm to the environment; eco-friendly is short for ecologically friendly

environment (in-VY-ruhn-muhnt)—the natural world of the land, water, and air

gratitude (GRAT-uh-tood)—a feeling of being thankful and grateful

landfill (LAND-fill)—an area where garbage is stacked and covered with dirt

papier-mache (PAY-pur muh-SHAY)—paper that has been soaked in glue; before hardening, this material can be molded into dolls, toys, furniture, and other objects

recycle (ree-SYE-kuhl) — to make used items into new products

template (TEM-plate)—a shape or pattern that you draw or cut around to make the same shape in paper, metal, or other materials

XXXX

Read More

Anton, Carrie. *Earth Smart Crafts: Transform Toss-away Items into Fun Accessories, Gifts, Room Décor, and More!* Middleton, Wis.: American Girl, 2009.

Chapman, Gillian, and Pam Robson. *Making Art with Paper.* Everyday Art. New York: PowerKids Press, 2008.

Sirrine, Carol. *Cool Crafts with Old Wrappers, Cans, and Bottles: Green Projects for Resourceful Kids.* Green Crafts. Mankato, Minn.: Capstone Press, 2010.

RECYCLE

Internet Sites

FactHound offers a safe, fun way to find Internet sites related to this book. All of the sites on FactHound have been researched by our staff.

Here's all you do:

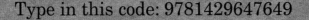

Visit *www.facthound.com*

Type in this code: 9781429647649

Index

About the Author

A Midwesterner-turned-California girl, Jen Jones loves to be in nature and is proud to be part of any project that makes our world a greener place! Jen is a Los Angeles-based writer who has authored more than 35 books for Capstone Press. Her stories have been published in magazines such as *American Cheerleader, Dance Spirit, Ohio Today,* and *Pilates Style.* She has also written for E! Online, MSN, and PBS Kids, as well as being a Web site producer for major talk shows such as *The Jenny Jones Show, The Sharon Osbourne Show,* and *The Larry Elder Show.* Jen is a member of the Society of Children's Book Writers and Illustrators.